Mel Bay Presents

GOOD TIMES,
HARD TIMES &
RAGTIMES

By Jerry Silverman

Cover illustration by Greg Ragland.

Contents

A Note From Jerry Silverman

The songs in this collection cover a period of about 25 years of tumultuous music making in America. The quarter century from 1890 to 1915 saw the usual rough-and-tumble election campaigns (and their equally rough-and-tumble campaign songs), a two-ocean war with Spain (with a new crop of sardonic soldiers' songs), a rise in social consciousness (labor unions, universal suffrage — and their agit-prop musical messages), an outpouring of lachrymose sentiment in flowery, moralistic, tear-jerking ballads, and finally — and from the musical point of view, the most significant — the coming of the age of ragtime.

There is a rich and varied cast of characters to be found herein: presidents William McKinley and Teddy Roosevelt, composers Scott Joplin, Joe Hill, Paul Dresser, George M. Cohan and others, striking workers and strikebreakers, soldiers, dancing girls, suckers and tough guys . . . all making music!

Hooray For Bill McKinley
And That Brave Rough Rider, Ted

By the 1900 election, ragtime was in full bloom.

3

never get up again; Mac and Ted – dy are going to
Kin – ley re – mained so mild, That as pres – i – dent he showed

win this po – li – ti – cal fight, And that is right! 'Cause the
his great a – bil – i – ty clean, And that's no dream. With a

ques – tions that are now pend – ing, And are caus – ing con – vul – sions of the
run – ning mate like Ted Roose – velt, That val – iant Rough Rid – er,

brain Can on – ly be set – tled by a cool – head – ed man like
free, He'll smash ev – 'ry par – ty that puts up a nom – i –

4

Mac. _____

nee. _____

Bil – ly Bry – an's cam-paign is
Too much brag – ging, I know, don't

end – ing, We'll have no Dem – o – crat to reign; For you

sound well, But we're gon – na make them look blue, On e –

know that good times is some – thing they al – ways lack, And that's a fact! But there's

lec – tion day what a hot time there'll be, Just you wait and see!

Chorus

no use in ar – gu – ing a – bout it, Bill Mc – Kin – ley's the win – ning thing, And it

there'll be a grand pro – ces – sion, And cake – walk – ing to beat the band, Such pa –

5

certain‑ly is too a – mus‑ing to see those Dem‑mies a– trying to sing. But when
rad – ing with torch‑lights blaz‑ing A–hail‑ing, good‑times for Un – cle Sam. And when

ev – ’ry thing ___ is ex – cite – ment, And that good old el – ec – tion’s won, And ’tis
ev – er I ___ meet a Dem–mie, I don’t care if he kills me

count–ed up, good old Mac and Ted–dy will have beat ’em six–teen to one. Oh, then

dead, I’ll yell, “Hoo–ray for Bill Mc – Kin–ley and that brave Rough Rid–er, Ted!”

Campaign Songs in an Election-Night Crowd.   *New York Public Library Picture Collection.*

Goodbye, My Party, Goodbye

Disillusioned by the election of Grover Cleveland in 1888, an ever-increasing number of Midwestern farmers simply gave up on the two-party system. They witnessed their hopes of making the prairie a land of plenty dispelled by an unhappy combination of drought and the depredations of the railroads, trusts, and moneylenders. By 1890, the Farmer's Alliance — a third party — was able to elect governors, senators, representatives and state legislators. Kansas led the way with a sweeping Populist victory. This is the song they sang.

It was no more than a year a-go,
hear aught else ___ I ne'er would go,
Good-bye, my par-ty, good-bye, ___
That I was in love with my par-ty so,
And just-like the rest I made a great blow,
Good-bye, my par-ty, good-bye. ___ To bye.
Sing-ing, bye-low, my par-ty, bye-low, my

par — ty, Sing — ing, by — low, my

par — ty,_____ Good—bye, my par—ty good—bye,_____

I was raised up in the kind of school,	And it made of me a "Kansas fool,"	The old party is on the downward track,	With a placard pinned upon his back,
Good-bye, my party, good-bye,	Good-bye, my party, good-bye,	Good-bye, my party, good-bye,	Good-bye, my party, good-bye,
That taught to bow to money rule,	When they found I was a willing tool.	Picking its teeth with a tariff tack,	That plainly states: "I will never go back."
Good-bye, my party, good-bye,	Good-bye, my party, good-bye.	Good-bye, my party, good-bye,	Good-bye, my party, good-bye.
Chorus	*Chorus*	*Chorus*	*Chorus*

Armed Republicans in the Kansas state house after driving out the Populists who had barricaded themselves inside (1893). *New York Public Library Picture Collection.*

Tammany

In 1891, the Reverend Charles Henry Parkhurst re-organized the Society for the Prevention of Crime in New York City. His principal target was the Democratic "machine," Tammany Hall. His efforts to clean up the city earned him the nickname "The Red Light Finder." He is not known to have had any other lasting effect.

Music by Gus Edward
Words by Vincent Bryan

Hi – a – wa – tha was an In – dian, so was Na – va – jo. Pale-face or – gan grind – ers killed them man – y moons a – go. But there is a band of In – dians that will nev – er die; When they're at the

On the Island of Manhattan
   By the bitter sea,
Lived this tribe of noble Red Men,
   Tribe of Tammany.
From the Totem of the Greenlight
   Wam-pum they would bring,
When their big Chief Man Behind,
    Would pass the pipe and sing: *Chorus*

Pale Face Preacher, "Red Light Finder,"
   To Manhattan came,
He was very old but he played
   Leapfrog just the same,
He side he would run Manhattan
   Like a Sunday school,
Made the village twice as bad
    As under Tammany rule.   *Chorus*

Pale Face Band of Pirates called
   "Reformers" made a fight,
Helped old "Red Light Finder"
   Put the Tam' my braves to flight.
Tammany came back and put this
   Pirate Band to rout,
Found the village treasure gone,
    "Reformers" cleaned it out. *Chorus*

The Full Dinner Pail

Once again in 1900 it was McKinley versus Bryan (as it had been in 1896). Riding on popular enthusiasm for the victories of the just-completed Spanish–American War, the team of McKinley–Roosevelt was swept into office.

Words by Henry Tyrrell
Music by Charles Puerner

There's a sound of march–ing mu – sic, and there's cheer–ing in the air, For the
tried and val–iant lead–er and a stan – dard that is fair, And we

con – test now is read–y to be – gin. We've a hope the bet – ter

man is going to win. There is Sil – ver Dol – lar Bry – an in the

Oh, the Dinner Pail is ample, and it's made of honest tin,
But it stands for what is worth its weight in gold.
There are honor and prosperity all snug and tight within,
And the courage to achieve and have and hold.
There is Silver Dollar Bryan, with repudiation coin,
He's a Jonah, let us throw him to the whale!
For the man that we select, and the man that we elect,
Is McKinley with the well-filled Dinner Pail. *Chorus*

When the war with Spain awakened all our spirit, *not* our fear,
And there came a time for action to be done,
Then our Army and our Navy to the roll call answered, "Here!"
And McKinley was the Man Behind the Gun.
There is Silver Dollar Bryan, with his anti-everything,
And his policy to murmur and to wail;
But when all the strife is past, Bryan, too, may break his fast,
From McKinley's over-flowing Dinner Pail. *Chorus*

We remember, yes, remember, not so very long ago,
When the times were hard and work was scarce, at that,
Now, what brought about the happy change, right well we also know,
Democratic years were lean, but ours are fat.
Down with Silver Dollar Bryan, with his promises of wind,
And his bill of fare so meagre and so stale:
We're contented with our lot, and we want the man we've got,
That's McKinley with the well-filled Dinner Pail. *Chorus*

Every Republican parade had a dinner pail. McKinley was re-elected by an 861,459 plurality, the biggest yet polled.
New York Public Library Picture Collection.

White House Blues

On September 6, 1901, while visiting the Pan–American Exhibition at Buffalo, New York, President William McKinley was shot at close range by Leon Czolgosz. After the world had been assured that the patient would do well and recover, he collapsed and died on the 14th. Vice-President Roosevelt immediately took the oath and assumed the office of the presidency.

McKinley, he hollered, McKinley, he squalled. The Doc said, "McKinley, I can't find the ball. You're bound to die, bound to die."

Oh it's look here you rascal, see what you done,
You shot my husband and I got your gun,
I'm takin' you back to Washington.

Oh the doc come a-running, took off his specs,
Said, "Mr. McKinley, better cash in your checks,
You're bound to die, bound to die."

Oh Roosevelt in the White House doin' his best,
McKinley in the graveyard takin' a rest,
He's gone, long gone.

The engine she whistled all down the line,
Blown' at every station, "McKinley is dyin',"
From Buffalo to Washington.

Roosevelt in the White House, drinkin' out a silver cup,
McKinley in the graveyard, he'll never wake up,
He's gone a long, old time.

The People's Jubilee

In the presidential election of 1892, the Populists' candidate, General James B. Weaver, received 22 electoral votes. This represented the high point of 19th-century American radicalism.

Words by C. S. White
Music by Henry C. Work
"Kingdom Coming"

Say __ work – ers, have you seen the boss – es, with the scared and pal – lid face, Go – in' down the al – ley some time this even – in' to __ find a hid – ing place. They saw the peo – ple cast their bal – lot and they knew their time had come; They

The working people are getting tired
Of having no home nor land;
So now, they say, to run this government
They are going to try their hand.
There's gold and silver in the White House cellar,
And the workers all want some,
For they know it will all be counted out
When the People's Party comes. *Chorus*

What's The Matter With Hanna?

Mark Hanna was the chairman of the Republican National Committee and McKinley's campaign director in 1896. Although he himself was not a candidate, he was favored with a "campaign" song. The "extra bandana" was a reference to the Democratic trademark of Cleveland's ill-fated campaign of 1888, when he was defeated by Harrison.

Words by Harry Denver
Music by Bertha C. Marshall

There's a ques – tion so old, it is stale we are told, But we'll

an – swer it now in the man – ner; With the com – ing of snow, we have

no flies, you know, And that's what's the mat – ter with Han – na,

Chorus

Oh, what's the mat – ter with Han– na? He is sing – ing a hap – py ho – san – na; He ___ knew what to do, so he did not boo– hoo, There is noth – ing the mat – ter with Han – na.

The fellows who kicked are sure to be licked,
And should carry an extra bandana;
They made a bad break and can't take the cake,
But that's not the matter with Hanna. *Chorus*

They had better go slow or a cyclone may blow,
If with silver they trim the old banner;
They will soon have enough of that bolt in a huff,
But all is serene with our Hanna. *Chorus*

Near the bright golden gate floats the good ship of state,
American patriots man her;
She is cleared for the fight, her crew is all right,
And that's what's the matter with Hanna. *Chorus*

21

New York Public Library Picture Collection.

Goodbye Teddy, You Must March, March, March

In 1904, in an effort to unseat Roosevelt, the Democrats nominated Chief Justice of the New York Court of Appeals, Alton B. Parker. It was no contest.

Words by Paul West
Music by John W. Bratton

flash – ing of the light – ning of his word.
good ship Con – sti – tu – tion, "All at sea."

At E – so – pus there's his hand up on the plough, And he
So with cheers and votes and glad – some heart and mind When No –

makes no sign of wa – ver–ing or doubt. Farm – er
vem – ber brings E – lect – ion Day a – round. We'll be

judge, no man de – ceiv–ing, Plain the truths that he's be – liev ing, And on
boom – ing things for Park–er And the pres – i – den – tial mark–er Will ob –

them he'd win the prize, or go with - out. Good

serve that Ted — dy's mar — gin can't be found.

Chorus G

morn — ing, Mis—ter Roos — evelt. per — mit _____

__ us to pre — sent _____ Just the man that we've se – lec—ted And who's

going to be e – lec—ted in your place as Pres — i — dent. _____ Go

FOR PRESIDENT:
THEO. ROOSEVELT.

LIBERTY
PROTECTION
PROSPERITY

"Protection, which guards & develops our Industries,
is a cardinal policy of the Republican party."
"We set Cuba free, governed the Island for 3 years,
& then gave it to the Cuban people with order restored."
"The great work of connecting the Pacific & Atlantic
by a Canal is at last begun by the Republican party."
"We firmley established the Gold Standard".
"Protection without injury to American
Agriculture, American Labor,
and American Industry."
COPYRIGHTED 1904 BY M. NEILS & ALLISON CHICAGO.

FOR VICE-PRESIDENT:
CHAS. W. FAIRBANKS.

REPUBLICAN

CANDIDATES.

New York Public Library Picture Collection.

27

You're All Right, Teddy

One of the many "Teddy" songs of 1904.

Words and Music by Cole and Johnson

The coun—try calls a—gain _____ For true and hon—est men, To
let us all u—nite, _____ And cast our bal—lots right, For

vote to save its hon—or and its fame; _____ So Ted—dy Roos—e—

velt, the man we name. Oh! you are all right Ted—dy! _____

You're the kind that we re—mem—ber; Don't _____ you wor—ry! We are with

Oh, Teddy is a man,
That's built upon a plan
To make the hearts of plucky men rejoice;
For when the game begins,
He goes right in and wins,
And that is why he is the people's choice. *Chorus*

Oh! you're a man indeed,
The kind of man we need,
The kind of man we need to hold the gap;
You've steered the country straight,
You've made the country great,
In fact, you've put the country on the map. *Chorus*

And when the country's cry
For men to fight and die
Resounded through the land from Washington,
Then Teddy didn't balk,
He didn't stop to talk,
But went and did his work at San Juan. *Chorus*

When Europe raised a fuss,
And tried to say to us:
"What? Dig through Panama, you never shall!"
Our Teddy said: "All right!
I'll think it over for a night."
Next day we got the Panama Canal. *Chorus*

Winning The Vote

By 1912, votes for women had become one of the central political issues of the day. The reference to Madison is due to the fact that this song was published by Busy World Publishing Company in Madison, Wisconsin (1912).

Words by Mrs. A. B. Smith

(Boys) I've been down to Mad–i–son to see the folks and sights; You'd
just as plain as my old hat, that's plain as plain can be, That

laugh, I'm sure, to hear them talk a – bout the wom–en's rights. Now, 'tis
if the wom–en want the vote, they'll

1.
2. get no help from me. Not from Joe, not from Joe, If he knows it,

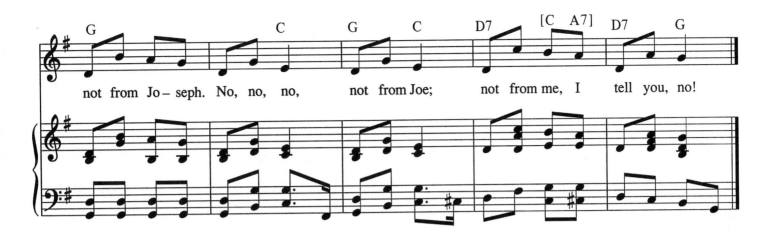

not from Jo-seph. No, no, no, not from Joe; not from me, I tell you, no!

Girls: Say, friend Joseph, why not we should vote as well as you?
    Are there no problems in the State that need our wisdom, too?
    We must pay our taxes same as you; as citizens be true,
    And if some wicked thing we do, to jail we're sent by you.
    Yes we are, same as you;
    And you know it, don't you, Joseph?
    Yes, you do, yet you boast:
    You'll not help us win the vote.

Boys: But dear women, can't you see, the home is your true sphere?
    Just think of going to the polls perhaps two times a year.
    You are wasting time you ought to use in sewing and at work,
    Your home neglected all those hours; would you such duties shirk?
    Help from Joe? Help from Joe?
    If he knows it, not from Joseph;
    No, no, no, not from Joe;
    Not from me, I tell you no!

Girls: Joseph, tell us something new - we're tired of that old song.
    We'll sew the seams and cook the meals, to vote won't take us long.
    We will help to clean house - the one too large for man to clean alone,
    The State and Nation, don't you see, when we the vote have won.
    Yes we will, and you'll help,
    For you'll need our help, friend Joseph.
    Yes you will, when we're in,
    So you'd better help us win.

Boys: You're just right - how blind I've been, I ne'er had seen it thus;
    'Tis true that taxes you must pay without a word of fuss.
    You are subject to the laws men made, and yet no word or note,
    Can you sing out where it will count. I'll help you win the vote!
    Yes, I will.

Girls: Thank you, Joe.

All: We'll together soon be voters.
    Yes we will, if you'll all
    Vote "Yes" at the polls next fall.

I'm A Suffragette

Words by M. Olive Drennan
Music by M. C. Hanford

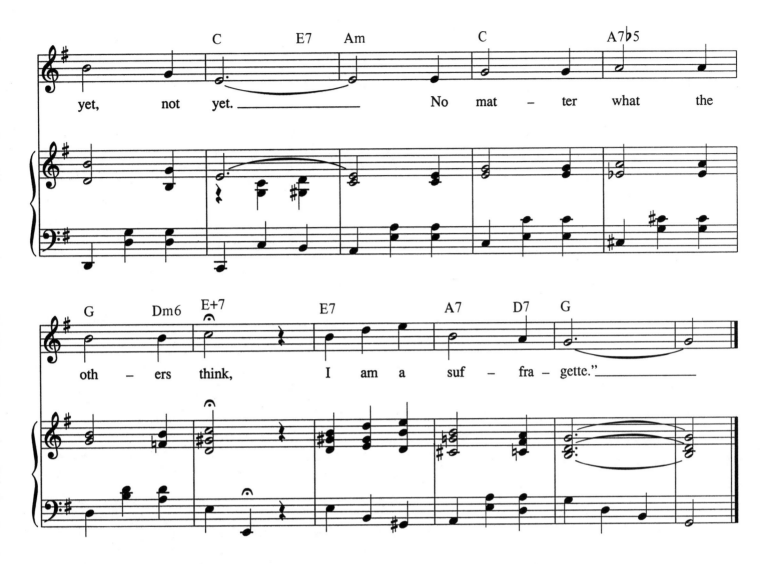

My papa does the voting
While mama does the work,
And when there is any shirking,
He is the one to shirk.   *Chorus*

And the children growing up,
Are starting in to school,
If the teacher's a gentleman,
They have to "mind the rule."   *Chorus*

Oh, the men make all the laws,
Which do we women fret,
But you should see those laws when we
At last our suffrage get.   *Chorus*

I have a dandy little beau,
He lives down in the town,
And when he asks me to "be his,"
I'll look at him and frown.   *Chorus*

Final chorus:
Yes, papa votes, but mama can't,
Oh no, not yet, not yet,
But I'll not marry any man
Till I my suffrage get.

Battleship Of Maine

On the 15th of February, 1898, the U.S. battleship *Maine* was destroyed in Havana harbor by an explosion, with a loss of 260 lives. The cry of "Remember the *Maine!*" was taken up all across the United States. On the 20th of April, President McKinley approved a resolution demanding the withdrawal of Spain from its Cuban colony. On the 22nd the President declared a blockade of Cuban ports. On the 24th the Spanish government declared war — a war that would stretch from Cuba all the way to the Philippines.

Mc – Kin – ley called for vol – un – teers, Then I got my gun. First
Span – iard I saw com – ing I dropped my gun and run; It was all a – bout __ that Bat – tle – ship of
Maine. At war with that great na – tion Spain. When I get back from Spain I want to
hon – or my name. It was all a – bout __ that Bat – tle – ship of Maine.

The blood was a-running
And I was running too,
I give my feet good exercise,
I had nothing else to do,
It was all about that **Battleship of Maine**. *Chorus*

When they were a-chasing me,
I fell down on my knees,
First thing I cast my eyes upon
Was a great big pot of peas,
It was all about that Battleship of Maine. *Chorus*

The peas they was greasy,
The meat it was fat,
The boys was fighting Spaniards
While I was fighting that,
It was all about that Battleship of Maine. *Chorus*

What kind of shoes
Do the rough riders wear,
Buttons on the side,
Cost five and a half a pair,
It was all about that Battleship of Maine. *Chorus*

What kind of shoes
Do the poor farmers wear,
Old brogans,
Cost a dollar a pair,
It was all about that Battleship of Maine. *Chorus*

Destruction of the U.S. Battleship *Maine* in Havana Harbor, February 15, 1898. *New York Public Library Picture Collection.*

A Dream

American soldiers in the Philippines indulging in a bit of "wishful drinking."

I dreamed that I dwelt on an isle of cracked ice, In the
midst of a lake of cham-pagne, _____ Where
bloomed the mint ju-leps in mea-dows of green, And
show-ers of lith-i-a rain. _____

I reclined on a divan of lager-beer foam,
With a pillow of froth for my head.
While the spray from a fountain of sparkling gin-fizz
Descended like dew on my bed.

From far-away mountains of crystalline ice,
A zephyr refreshing and cool
Came wafting the incense of sweet muscatel
That sparkled in many a pool.

My senses were soothed by the soft, purling song
Of a brooklet of pousse-café
That rippled along over pebbles of snow
To a river of absinth frappé.

Then lulled by the music of tinkling glass
From the schooners that danced on the deep,
I dreamily sipped a high-ball or two,
And languidly floated to sleep.

And then I awoke on a bed full of rocks,
With a bolster as hard as a brick,
A wrench in my neck, a rack in my head,
And a stomach detestably sick.

With sand in my eyes and a grit in my throat
Where the taste of last evening still clung.
I felt a bath towel stuffed into my mouth,
Which I afterwards found was my tongue.

And I groped for the thread of the evening before
In the mystified maze of my brain,
Until a great light burst upon me at last-
"I'm Off of the Wagon Again."

New York Public Library Picture Collection.

A Rookie

He was a lu-lu, you bet. _____ When he stood on his head, These words gent-ly said; "I'll be a sec-ond George Wash-ing-ton yet." _____

At Frisco he did land;
They took him in hand;
All the old bucks soon gathered 'round.
"Say, when did you enlist?"
"Oh, give me your fist!"
"You'll take on again, I'll be bound."
"I've a blanket to sell;
It will fit you quite well.
You may take it – the whole or a piece."
"I've a dress coat to trade,
And a helmet unmade;
It will do you for kitchen police." *Chorus*

Now they gave him a gun,
And the "Top" said, "My son,
Come, heel-ball this musket up bright.
In a few days or more
You'll be wilted in gore
When you go those fierce Moros to fight.
There'll be blood flowing free;
You'll be right there to see;
We'll send you right up to the front.
You need have no fear;
If you get scalped, my dear,
You'll be pensioned – eight dollars per month." *Chorus*

Now they scared him so bad
He blew in all he had
And went on a drunk with good will.
The "Top" did report,
"There's one private short."
When he showed up he went to the mill.
The proceedings, we find,
Was a ten dollars blind.
It was ten dollars less to blow foam.
That was long years ago,
And that rookie, you know,
Is now in the old soldiers' home. *Chorus*

In Mindanao

Admiral Dewey sailed his fleet into Manila harbor in May 1898. By August the "liberation" of the Philippines was complete. Almost immediately, friction and then hostilities broke out between the American forces and the Philippine rebel leader Emilio Aguinaldo. For the next three years there was fighting between the U.S. Army and Aguinaldo's troops. With the capture of Aguinaldo on March 23, 1901, the "Philippine Insurrection" was effectively terminated. This song describes the difficulties the U.S. Army encountered in building a strategic road on the island of Mindanao.

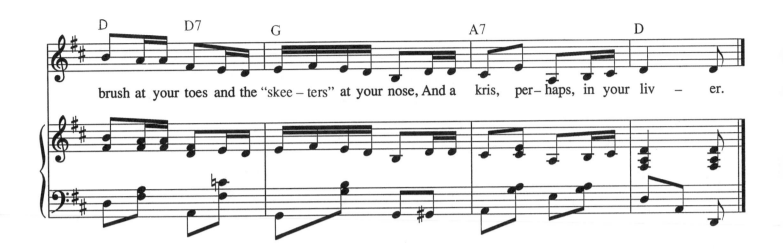

brush at your toes and the "skee – ters" at your nose, And a kris, per–haps, in your liv – er.

We've the dhobee-itch and the hamstring hitch,
    The jimjams and the fever;
The ping-pong wrist and the bolo fist,
    And a bumpus on the liver.
We're going up to Lake Lanao,
    To the town they call Marahui;
When the road is built and the Moros "kilt,"
    There'll none of us be sorry.

We're blasting stumps and grading bumps;
    Our hands and backs are sore, oh!
We work all day just dreaming of our pay,
    And damn the husky Moros!
When you're pulled from bed with a great big head,
    And a weakness o'er you stealing;
The sick report is a fine resort
    To cure that tired feeling.

New York Public Library Picture Collection.

Stung Right

Joe Hill (1879–1915) was the composer of dozens of militant labor and political songs during the early years of the 20th century. Here he takes ironic aim not only at the naive young man who joins the navy "to see the world," but also at the Armour meat packing company, whose spoiled cans of meat supplied to U.S. forces were the cause of a notorious scandal during the Spanish–American War.

By Joe Hill

As I was hik – ing 'round the town to find a job one day, I
take a trip a – round the world in Un – cle Sam – my's fleet, I

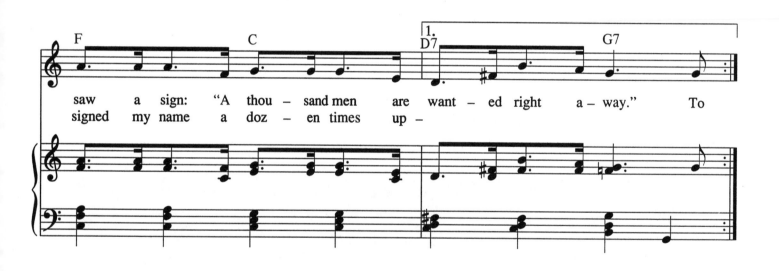

saw a sign: "A thou – sand men are want – ed right a – way." To
signed my name a doz – en times up –

Chorus

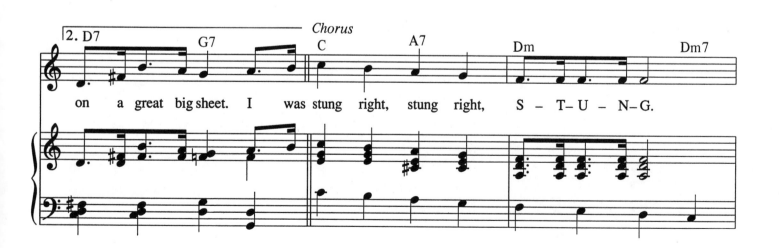

2. on a great big sheet. I was stung right, stung right, S – T–U – N–G.

The man, he said, "The U.S. Fleet, it is no place for slaves,
For everything you to do is stand and watch the waves!"
But in the morn, at five o'clock, they woke me from my snooze,
To scrub the deck and polish brass, and shine the captain's shoes! *Chorus*

One day a dude in uniform to me began to shout;
I simply plugged him in the jaw, and knocked him down and out;
They slammed me right in irons then and said, "You are a case."
On bread and water then I lived for twenty-seven days. *Chorus*

One day the captain said, "Today I'll show you something nice,
All hands line up, we'll go ashore and do some exercise."
He made us run for seven miles as fast as we could run,
And with a packing on our back that weighed a half a ton. *Chorus*

Some time ago when Uncle Sam he had a war with Spain,
And many of the boys in blue were in the battle slain,
Not all were killed by bullets, though; no, not by any means,
The biggest part that died were killed by Armour's Pork and Beans. *Chorus*

Bacon On The Rind

A sol – dier in the cav – al – ry lay on a can – vas bunk. On a
soap – box there be – side him lay a hunk of arm–y punk; And as he
chewed a – way so bus–y,_____ his face turned ash – en gray, For the

cut to sign for 4th verse 𝄋

sol – dier boy was dy – ing in the Is – land far a – way. As his

46

And as he lay there gasping with the moments flying fast,
He tried to chew a rubber boot 'fore life went out at last.
And he said to his comrades, "Bring me a box of soap,
For they eat it in the frozen north, and where there is life there is hope.
But, Charlie dear, I greatly fear, my race is almost run,
Life's feeble spark will be snuffed out ere the setting of the sun.
Take a message and a token to the dear ones left behind,
And say I starved on Bacon, Army Bacon on the Rind."

That evening just at twilight, as the flag slid down the pole,
We bowed our heads in silence for the parting soul;
But that night beside the camp-fire you could hear his comrades say,
"If he'd had a soldier's ration he'd be alive today.
A curse on the man who did it, tho' with coin his purse be lined,
May he starve on Prunes and Bacon, Army Bacon on the Rind."
In a trim New England cottage sits a mother old and gray.
In her hand she holds a letter that came by mail that day.

And as she sits there reading, her eyes are filled with tears,
For the letter brings the tidings that every mother fears.
It tells how in the Islands her darling met his death,
Fighting for flag and country midst the battle's frenzied breath;
But it don't tell how it happened, and perhaps the Fates are kind,
For her darling starved on Bacon, Army Bacon on the Rind.

The Brooklyn Strike

In 1895, motormen and other employees of the Putnam Avenue–Halsey Street went out on strike for a 25-cent-a-day increase in wages. When imported strikebreakers failed to split the ranks, Brooklyn Major Charles A. Shieren (Brooklyn was a city then) called out the militia. In the ensuing violence, a number of strikers and sympathizers were injured, and some were killed. The strike was broken.

can the pam — pered mil – lion — aires the spir – it in us break, _____ The fame of our fair ci – ty _____ is clear – ly now at stake. _____

The soulless corporations should know
　this lesson pat
A fair day's work for a fair day's pay is
　what we're aiming at
They cannot run their trolley lines with
　lazy dudes and tramps
With safety to the public long, who
　detest vile scabs and scamps. *Chorus*

The railroad men with one accord are
　in this fight to stay
They ask for what is but their right
　and right will win always
The public all are with them too for
　weal or woe or die
And workingmen throughout the land
　Will heed their pleading cry. *Chorus*

51

Buddy, Won't You Roll Down The Line?

In the 1880s Southern miners tried to organize the Knights of Labor. In Tennessee their efforts were thwarted by the presence in the mines of thousands of convicts, leased at $60 a head by the state government to the coal companies.

Way back yon-der in Ten-nes-see they leased the con-victs out,____
la-bor fought-a-gainst it, To win it took some time,____

____ They put them work-ing in the mines a-gainst free la-bor stout.
____ But while the lease was in ef-fect, they

Free made them rise and shine. Bud-dy, won't you roll down ____ the

line? Bud-dy, won't you roll down ____ the line? _____ Yon-der comes my

52

Every Monday morning they get you out on time,
March you down to Lone Rock just to look into that mine.
March you down to Lone Rock to look into that hole,
Very last words the captain says, "You better get your pole." *Chorus*

The beans they are half done, the bread is not so well,
The meat it is all burnt up and the coffee's black as heck,
But when you get your task done, you're glad to come to call,
For anything you get to eat, it tastes good done or raw. *Chorus*

Pay Day At Coal Creek

Coal Creek, Tennessee — now named Lake City — was the site of the Coal Creek Rebellion of 1891, in which the miners fought at gun point against the strikebreaking policy of leased convict-labor (described in the previous song).

at Coal Creek _ to – mor – row. _

Pay day, pay day, oh, pay day,
Pay day don't come at Coal Creek no more,
Pay day don't come to more.

Bye-bye, bye-bye, oh bye-bye,
Bye-bye, my woman, I'm gone,
Bye-bye, my woman, I'm gone.

You'll miss me, you'll miss me, you'll miss me,
You'll miss me when I'm gone,
You'll miss me when I'm gone.

I'm a poor boy, I'm a poor boy, I'm a poor boy,
I'm a poor boy and a long ways from home,
I'm a poor boy and a long ways from home.

Easy rider, oh, easy rider, oh, easy rider,
Oh, easy rider, but you'll leave the rail some time,
Oh, easy rider, but you'll leave the rail some time.

Pay day, pay day, oh, pay day,
Pay day don't come at Coal Creek no more,
Pay day don't come no more.

New York Public Library Picture Collection.

55

Trouble Down At Homestead

The famous Homestead steel strike took place in 1892 in the little town of Homestead, near Pittsburgh. The strike lasted for 143 long and bitter days — miners against Andrew Carnegie. Pinkerton agents were called in as strikebreakers, and eventually the Pennsylvania militia was ordered into the fray.

See that band of sturdy workingmen
   start at the break of day
With determination in their face
   that's surely meant to say:
"No man can drive us from our homes
   for which we've toiled so long,
No man can take our places
   for here's where we belong." *Chorus*

A woman with a rifle
   and her husband in the crowd,
She handed him the weapon,
   they cheered her long and loud;
He kissed her, then said:
   "Mary, go home till we are through."
She answered: "No, if you must die,
   my place is here with you." *Chorus*

See that band of tramp detectives
   come without authority,
Like thieves at night while decent men
   are sleeping peacefully;
Would you wonder that our decent men
   with indignation burn,
The lowly worm that crawls the earth
   when tread upon will turn. *Chorus*

57

The Factory Girl

It is a matter of history that the industrial age was ushered in by the first weaving factories, the forerunners of today's mammoth textile industry. And to the cities of Massachusetts — to Lawrence and Lowell and the other textile centers — came the fresh young farm girls looking for work. . . . Conditions in these early factories, where a fourteen-hour work day was the norm, were bad enough for the city girl . . . but to the country girl, used to the smell of trees and grass and the closeness of sky and earth, the textile factories were structures of damnation. (*Sing Out,* Vol. 9, No. 2, Fall 1959)

No more shall I hear the bosses say,
"Girls, you'd better daulf."
No more shall I hear those bosses say,
"Spinners, you'd better clean off." *Chorus*

No more shall I hear the drummer wheels
A-rolling over my head.
When factories are hard at work,
I'll be in my bed. *Chorus*

No more shall I hear the whistle blow
To call me up so soon.
No more shall I hear the whistle blow
To call me from my home. *Chorus*

No more shall I see the super come,
All dressed up so proud;
For I know I'll marry a country boy
Before the year is out. *Chorus*

No more shall I wear the old black dress,
Greasy all around.
No more shall I wear the old black bonnet,
With holes all in the crown. *Chorus*

New York Public Library Picture Collection.

Mister Block

Joe Hill was the song-writing voice of the International Workers of the World. In 1910 many of his songs appeared in the I.W.W. songbook — *Songs to Fan the Flames of Discontent*. His songs were sung in union halls, street rallies and on countless picket lines. "Mr. Block" is a "teaching song." Though "he is a common worker," Mr. Block does not fully comprehend the nature of the class struggle. He makes one error after another. Joe Hill hoped his audience would benefit from Mr. Block's follies and *not* do likewise.

By Joe Hill

lake. Kind–ly do that for Lib – er – ty's sake. _____

Yes, Mr. Block is lucky; he found a job, by gee!
The shark got seven dollars, for job add fare and fee.
They shipped him to a desert and dumped him with his truck,
But when he tried to find his job, he sure was out of luck.
He shouted, "That's too raw,
I'll fix them with the law!" *Chorus*

Block hiked back to the city, but wasn't doing well.
He said, "I'll join the union – the great A.F. of L."
He got a job next morning, got fired in the night,
He said, "I'll see Sam Gompers and he'll fix that foreman right."
Sam Gompers said, "You see,
You've got our sympathy." *Chorus*

Election Day he shouted, "A Socialist for Mayor!"
The "comrade" got elected, he happy was for fair.
But after the election, he got an awful shock;
A great big socialistic "bull" did rap him on the block.
And Comrade Block did sob,
"I helped him to his job." *Chorus*

The money kings in Cuba blew up the gunboat *Maine,*
But Block got awful angry and blamed it all on Spain.
He went right in the battle and there he lost his leg,
And now he's peddling shoestrings and is walking on a peg.
He shouts, "Remember *Maine,*
Hurrah! To hell with Spain!" *Chorus*

Poor Block he died one evening, I'm very glad to state;
He climbed the golden ladder up to the pearly gate.
He said, "Oh, Mr. Peter, one word I'd like to tell,
I'd like to meet the Astorbilts and John D. Rockefell."
Old Pete said, "Is that so?
You'll meet them down below." *Chorus*

Clothing workers' strike.   *New York Public Library Picture Collection.*

Bread And Roses

New Year's Day, 1912, ushered in one of the most historic struggles in the history of the American working class. On that cold January first, the textile workers of Lawrence, Massachusetts, began a nine-week strike which shook the very foundations of the Bay State and had national repercussions. In its last session, the Massachusetts State Legislature, after tremendous pressure from the workers, had finally passed a law limiting the working hours of children under the age of 18 to 54 hours a week. Needless to say, the huge textile corporations had viciously opposed the law. As an act of retaliation, the employers cut the working hours of all employees to 54 hours a week, with a commensurate cut in wages, of course. The workers in the Lawrence factories, some 35,000 of them, answered this with a complete walk-out.... During a parade through Lawrence, a group of women workers carried banners proclaiming "Bread and Roses!" This poetic presentation of the demands of women workers for equal pay for equal work, together with special consideration as women, echoed throughout the country. (*Sing Out,* Vol. 2, No. 7, January 1952)

Music by Martha Coleman
Words by James Oppenheim

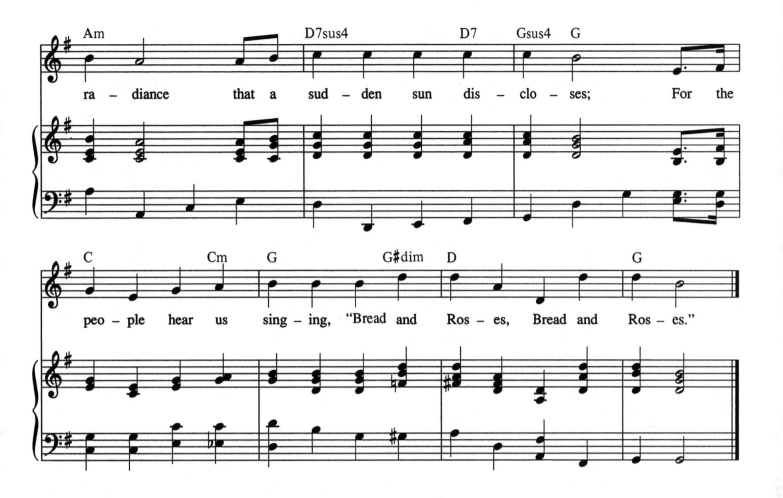

As we come marching, marching, we battle too, for men,
For they are women's children and we mother them again.
Our lives shall not be sweated from birth until life closes.
Hearts starve as well as bodies:
Give us bread, but give us roses.

As we come marching, marching, unnumbered women dead
Go crying through our singing their ancient song of bread.
Small art and love and beauty their drudging spirits knew.
Yes, it is bread that we fight for,
But we fight for roses, too.

As we come marching, marching, we bring the Greater Days,
The rising of the women means the rising of the race.
No more the drudge and idler, ten that toil where one reposes,
But a sharing of life's glories,
Bread and Roses, Bread and Roses.

The Popular Wobbly

The Industrial Workers of the World was founded in 1905. Its main influence was felt in the Western states, where it won the allegiance of tens of thousands of longshoremen, copper miners and unskilled workers of many trades. Its members were called "Wobblies." T-Bone Slim was the nom de Wobbly of a Chicago meat packer.

Words by T-Bone Slim

I'm as mild – man–nered man as can be, _____ And I've
nev – er done them harm as I can see. _____ Still on
me they put a ban, And they threw me in the can, They go
wild, simp – ly wild o – ver me. _____

They accuse me of rascality,
But I can't see why they always pick on me.
I'm as gentle as a lamb,
But they take me for a ram,
They go wild, simply wild over me.

Oh the "bull" he went wild over me,
And he held his gun where everyone could see.
He was breathing rather hard
When he saw my union card,
He went wild, simply wild over me.

Then the judge he went wild over me,
And I plainly saw we never could agree.
So I let "his Nibs" obey
What his conscience had to say,
He went wild, simply wild over me.

Oh the jailer he went wild over me,
And he locked me up and threw away the key.
It seems to be the rage,
So they keep me in a cage,
They go wild, simply wild over me.

They go wild, simply wild over me,
I'm referring to the bedbug and the flea.
They disturb my slumber deep,
And I murmur in my sleep,
They go wild, simply wild over me.

Will the roses grow wild over me,
When I'm gone into the land that is to be?
When my soul and body part,
In the stillness of my heart,
Will the roses grow wild over me?

New York Public Library Picture Collection.

The Preacher And The Slave

In this 1911 song, Joe Hill shows a down-to-earth attitude toward pie-in-the-sky.

Words by Joe Hill
Music: *The Sweet Bye And Bye*

pray,   live on hay,   you'll get pie in the sky when you die."

(that's a lie)

And the starvation army they play,
And they sing and they clap and they pray.
'Til they get all your coin on the drum,
Then they'll tell you when you're on the bum: *Chorus*

Holy Rollers and Jumpers come out,
And they holler, they jump and they shout.
"Give your money to Jesus," they say,
"He will cure all diseases today." *Chorus*

If you fight hard for children and wife—
Try to get something good in this life—
You're a sinner and bad man, they tell,
When you die you will sure go to hell. *Chorus*

Workingmen of all countries unite,
Side by side we for freedom will fight!
When the world and its wealth we have gained,
To the grafters we'll sing this refrain: *Chorus*

Final Chorus:
"You will eat, bye and bye,
When you've learned how to cook and to fry.
Chop some wood, 'twill do you good,
And you'll eat in the sweet bye and bye."

Scissor Bill

"Scissor Bill," like "Mr. Block," is another character who refuses to understand his class interests as a working man.
Joe Hill did not think too much of either — and consigned them both to a watery grave.

By Joe Hill

ev-'ry place.___ Scis-sor Bill,__ he is a lit-tle dip-py; Scis-sor Bill, he

has a fun-ny face. Scis-sor Bill___ should drown in Mis-si-sip-pi – He

is the mis-sing link that Dar-win tried___ to trace.___

Don't try to talk your union dope to Scissor Bill,
He says he never organized and never will.
He always will be satisfied until he's dead,
With coffee and a doughnut and a lousy old bed.
And Bill he says he'll get rewarded a thousandfold,
When he gets up to Heaven on the streets of gold;
But I don't care who knows it and right here I'll tell,
If Scissor Bill is going to Heaven, I will go to Hell.
    Scissor Bill, he wouldn't join the union;
    Scissor Bill, he says, "Not me, by heck!"
    Scissor Bill, gets his reward in Heaven,
    Oh, sure, he'll get it, but he'll get it in the neck.

The Rebel Girl

Imprisoned, and about to be executed by firing squad in Salt Lake City for murder — a crime of which his many supporters claimed he was innocent — Joe Hill found time to write to Elizabeth Gurley Flynn — "The Rebel Girl":

Elizabeth Gurley Flynn
511 - 134th
N. Y. City
Dear Friend Gurley:

Salt Lake City
Nov. 18, 1915
10 P. M.

    I have been saying Goodbye so much now that it is becoming monotonous but I just can not help to send you a few more lines because you have been more to me than a Fellow Worker. You have been an inspiration and when I composed The Rebel Girl you was right there and helped me all the time. As you furnished the idea I will now that I am gone give you all the credit for that song, and be sure to locate a few more Rebel Girls like yourself, because they are needed and needed badly . . . With a warm handshake across the continent and a last fond Goodbye to all I remain Yours As Ever

Joe Hill

By Joe Hill

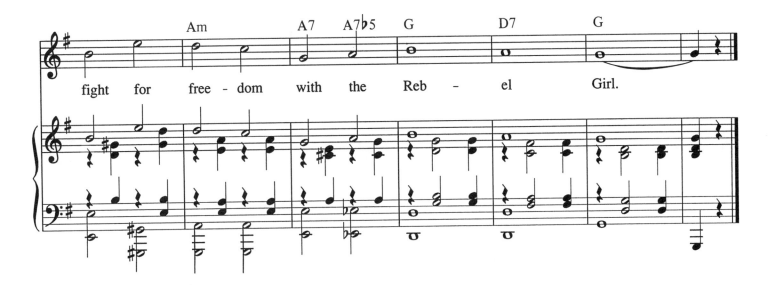

fight for free-dom with the Reb - el Girl.

A 1916 militant urges trolley strikers' wives not to let their men weaken.
New York Public Library Picture Collection.

The New Bully Song

By Charles E. Trevathan

I'm going down the street with my ax in my hand,
I'm looking for that bully and I'll sweep him off this land,
I'm a-looking for that bully and he must be found.
I'll take 'long my razor, I'm going to carve him deep,
And when I see that bully, I'll lay him down to sleep,
I'm looking for that bully and he must be found *Chorus*

I went to a wingin' down at Parson Jones,
Took along my trusty blade to carve that fella's bones,
Just a-looking for that bully, hear his groans.
I walked in the front door, the men were prancing high,
For that levee fella I skinned my foxy eye,
Just a-looking for that bully but he wasn't nigh *Chorus*

I asked Miss Pansy Blossom if she would wing a reel,
She says, "Law, Mr. Johnsing, how high you make me feel."
Then you ought to see me shake my sugar heel.
I rose up like a black cloud and took a look around,
There was that new bully standing on the ground.
I've been looking for you, fella, and I've got you found. *Chorus*

When I got through with bully, a doctor and a nurse
Weren't no good to that man, so they put him in a hearse,
A cyclone couldn't have tore him up much worse.
You don't hear 'bout that fella that treated folks so free,
Go down upon the levee and his face you'll never see,
There's only one boss bully, and that one is me. *Chorus*

When you see me coming, hoist your windows high,
When you see me going, hang your heads and cry,
I'm a-looking for that bully and he must die.
My madness is a-rising and I'm not going to get left,
I'm getting so bad that I'm askeered of myself,
I was looking for that bully, now he's on the shelf. *Chorus*

Bob Cole and J. Rosamond Johnson, writers of the first true black operettas.
New York Public Library Picture Collection.

Joe Turner

When Pete Turney became the governor of Tennessee in 1892, he made his brother Joe the "long-chain man." It was Joe Turney's job to transport convicts from Memphis to the Nashville penitentiary. So when Joe Turney came to town, it was bye-bye for some woman's man. Through a typical folk metamorphosis, his name was changed to Joe Turner. This is, perhaps, the oldest recorded blues. It is sometimes referred to as the "Granddaddy of the Blues."

Moderate

He come with forty links of chain.
He come with forty links of chain. (Oh, Lordy)
Got my man and gone.

They tell me Joe Turner's come and gone.
They tell me Joe Turner's come and gone. (Oh, Lordy)
Done left me here to sing this song.

Come like he never come before.
Come like he never come before.   (Oh, Lordy)
Got my man and gone.

Duncan And Brady

Brady, he lit out toward the door,
Duncan pulled out his big forty-four.
He shot him once and he shot him twice
Saying, "That'll take care of your cheatin' at dice." *Chorus*

Brady, he staggered and fell to the ground.
Duncan said, "You're on your last go 'round.
I told you a dozen times or more,
And now you lie dead on the barroom floor." *Chorus*

Brady went to hell lookin' mighty curious,
The devil says, "Where you from?" "East St. Louis."
"Well, pull off your coat and step this way,
For I've been expecting you every day!" *Chorus*

When the girls heard that Brady was dead
They went up home and put on red,
And came down town singin' this song:
"Brady's struttin' in hell with his Stetson on!" *Chorus*

Final Chorus:
Brady, oh, where you at?
Brady, where you at?
Brady, where you at?
Just a-struttin' in hell with his Stetson hat!

Original Rags

In 1899, Scott Joplin published this — his first rag. It was not uncommon for him, and others, to set words to his popular rags. I have followed this tradition in the next five ragtime songs.

Music by Scott Joplin
Words by Jerry Silverman

Section I

I feel like sing- ing this song,__ it does-n't
tum - ble right out,__ they kind of

take ve- ry long,__ you know I real- ly just can't seem to stop, It was-n't so long a- go,__ a gen- er-
stum-ble a-bout__ but un - der- neath is a good sol- id bass. The sec-ret is in the swing__ the syn- co-

a - tion or so__ that pia-no rag-time__ was first played by Scott Jop- lin. Since "nine-ty nine," his mu-sic's
pa-tion's the thing, A sim-ple mat-ter of a six - teenth dis - place-ment. Don't start to squawk__ at all this

mel-lowed like wine, It's brought, us shuffles and shim-mies- and shags;
tech - ni - cal talk, The main thing, is not to let the beat drag.

And bright syn-co- pa-tion

To Section IV
after 3rd ending

sweep-ing the na - tion, with the O - ri - gi - nal Rags. The notes just Rags
learn how to wing it

Section II

Section III

1st time **p**
2nd time **f**

Section IV
Brilliant

Repeat from 𝄋
then go to Section IV

Heliotrope Bouquet

**Music by Scott Joplin
and Louis Chauvin
Words by Jerry Silverman**

Slow march tempo

It was once on a sum- mer's day, Long a-go, far__ a- way, I heard a fel – low play He- li- o- trope__ Bou-quet.

He played those i- vo- ries like a cool sum- mer breeze. (I can't re- mem- ber his name.) But I just loved the mel- o- dy, and the strange har- mo- ny; Oh, what it did__ to me! So I re-solved that I would

joy knew no bounds;___ At each new turn twist and wig-gle, as rag-time re-sounds.___ He-li-o-
trope Bou – quet ___ came my way, ___ Now it's here to stay.

90

Peacherine Rag

Music by Scott Joplin
Words by Jerry Silverman

Guitarists may play chords in parentheses, with capo on 3rd fret.
The diminished chords remain the same.

sing it, shout it can't live with out it: I mean, The Peach er-ine. Rag, You've got to Rag.
so con - ten - ted that they in-vent ed that good old Peach er-ine.

93

94

Rag-Time Dance

Music by Scott Joplin
Words by Jerry Silverman

Guitarists may play chords in parentheses, with capo on 3rd fret.
The diminished chords remain the **same**.

all bow low,_ It's just as eas–y as eas–y can be._
in a trance, Just watch and see how their con-fidence grows_

Now__ you prom-en -ade your la–dy
Walk - ing for that cake is real–ly

home– ward — And go on to the next beau–ty that you see.
some– thing,_ And who will win it, well, good – ness on – ly

knows.

NOTICE: To get the desired effect of "Stop Time," the pianist will please **Stamp** the heel of one foot heavily upon the floor at the word "Stamp." Do not raise the toe from the floor while stamping. [Scott Joplin]

97

The Easy Winners

Music by Scott Joplin
Words by Jerry Silverman

Guitarists may play chords in parentheses, with capo on 1st fret.

Joplin, he changed our way of life, just with a few lit-tle notes.__ All the old songs were a-
Ragtime is eas-y to lis-ten to, eas-y to play and to sing. __ All there is to do is

top-plin', they just did-n't stand a chance, his mu-sic won all the votes.____ All dressed in
keep time, the feel-ing will come to you__ just let the mel-o-dy swing.____ And then in

pop-lin and crin-o-line, all the gals had beaux in swal-low-tail coats.__ As they
no time you'll do what you have to do__ you'll get the hang of the thing.__ And then

danced for their din-ners, they all ___ were Eas-y Win-ners, And hap-pi-ly sowed their wild oats.   King.
all   you song spin-ners will be ___ the Eas-y Win-ners, For rag-time will al-ways be

102

New York Public Library Picture Collection.

With All Her Faults I Love Her Still

By Monroe H. Rosenfeld

1. With all her faults I love her still_____ And e-ven though the world should
2. way one sum-mer day, _____ And nev-er came a-gain to
3. faults I love her still,_____ Al-though her love for me is

scorn; _____ No love like hers, _____ my heart can thrill, _____ Al-
me._____ And since that day _____ I long and pray _____ That
dead._____ In ev-'ry dream _____ Her smile doth beam, _____ Nor

though she's made my heart_____ for-lorn! Tho' oth-er hearts have won her
I my pass life's drear-y sea! I see her now as first we
care I what the world_____ hath said! I know that she'll re-turn a-

love, I bear for her no dreams of ill. Her face to
met, The sun-light shin-ing o'er her brow. The days were
gain, Al-though her face no more I greet. And when this

You're The Flower Of My Heart, Sweet Adeline

Words by Richard H. Gerard
Music by Harry Armstrong

I can see your smiling face as when wandered
Down by the brookside, just you and I.
And it seems so real at times that I awaken
To find all vanished, a dream gone by.
If we meet sometime in after years, my darling,
I trust that I will find your your love still mine.
Altho' my heart is sad and clouds above are hov'ring,
The sun again, love, for me would shine.   *Chorus*

Mrs. William Vanderbuilt at her fancy dress ball, 1883.   *New York Public Library Picture Collection.*

A Bird In A Gilded Cage

Words by Arthur J. Lamb
Music by Harry von Tilzer

1. The ball-room was filled with fashion's throng, It shone with a thou-sand lights;_____ And there was a wo-man who passed a-long, The fair-est of all the sights._____ A girl to her lov-er then soft-ly sighed, "There's

2. I stood in a church-yard just at eve, When sun-set a-dorned the west;_____ And looked at the peo-ple who'd come to grieve. For loved ones now laid at rest._____ A tall mar-ble mon-u-ment marked the grave of_____

The Titanic

Oh, they built the ship Ti – tan – ic to sail the o - cean blue, And they

thought they had a ship that the wa - ter would nev- er go through; But the

Lord's al - migh - ty hand said that ship would nev - er land, It was

Chorus

sad __ when that great __ ship went down. It was sad, it was

sad, It was sad when that great __ ship went down

(to the bot-tom of the)

hus – bands and wives, lit – tle chil – dren lost their lives. It was

sad ____ when that great ____ ship went down.

Oh, they sailed from England's shore
'Bout a thousand miles or more,
When the rich refused to associate with the poor
So, they put them down below,
Where they'd be the first to go,
It was sad when that great ship went down. *Chorus*

Oh, the boat was full of sin,
And the sides about to burst,
When the captain shouted, "Women and children first!"
Oh, the captain tried to wire,
But the lines were all on fire,
It was sad when that great ship went down. *Chorus*

Oh, they swung the lifeboats out
O'er the deep and raging sea,
And the band struck up with "A-nearer, My God, to Thee."
Little children wept and cried,
As the waves swept o'er the side.
It was sad when that great ship went down. *Chorus*

After The Ball

By Charles K. Harris

bies, have you no home?" _____ "I had a

sweet – heart, years, a – go;_____ Where

she is now, pet, you will soon know._____

List to the sto – ry, I'll tell it all,_____

"Bright lights were flashing
In the grand ballroom,
Softly the music, playing sweet tunes,
There came my sweetheart,
My love, my own,
"I wish some water; leave me alone."
When I returned, dear, there stood a man,
Kissing my sweetheart, as lovers can.
Down fell the glass, pet,
Broken, that's all,
Just as my heart was, after the ball. *Chorus*

Long years have passed, child;
I've never wed,
True to my lost love, though she is dead.
She tried to tell me,
Tried to explain;
I would not listen, pleadings were vain.
One day a letter came from that man;
He was her brother, the letter ran,
That's why I'm lonely,
No home at all;
I broke her heart, pet, after the ball. *Chorus*

121

On The Banks Of The Wabash, Far Away

By Paul Dresser

123

New York Public Library Picture Collection.

She Is More To Be Pitied Than Censured

By William B. Gray

1. At the old con-cert hall on the Bow-'ry,_____ 'Round a ta-ble were
2. There's an old-fash-ioned church 'round the cor-ner,_____ Where the neigh-bors all

seat-ed one night,_____ A ___ crowd of young fel-lows ca-
gath-ered one day,_____ While the par-son was preach-ing a

rous-ing,_____ With ___ them life seemed cheer-ful and bright. _____
ser-mon _____ O'er a soul that had just passed a-way. _____

At the ver-y next ta-ble was seat-ed _____ A ___
'Twas this same way-ward girl from the Bow-'ry,_____ Who a

I Lie In The American Land

In stark contrast to the music-hall ballads of the Gay '90s is this Slovak miner's song from the coal fields of Pennsylvania.

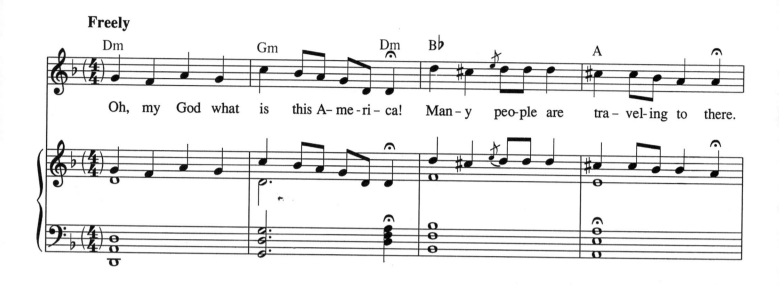

Oh, my God what is this A- me-ri - ca! Man - y peo-ple are tra - vel-ing to there.

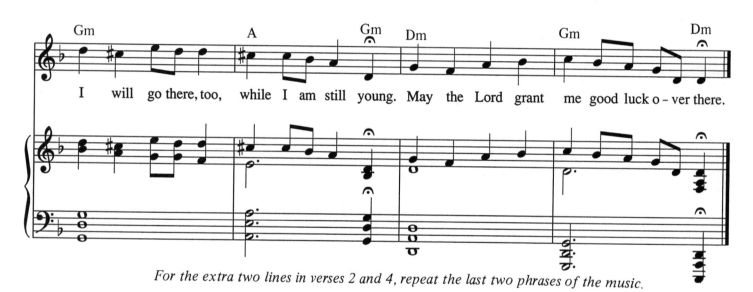

I will go there, too, while I am still young. May the Lord grant me good luck o - ver there.

For the extra two lines in verses 2 and 4, repeat the last two phrases of the music.

I'll return to you if I don't get killed.
I will send you news from that far-off land.
And when you receive word from me, my dear.
Put your things in order, and do not fear.
Mount a raven-black steel — don't look behind.
Quickly fly to me, oh dear soul of mine.

But when in McKeesport she did arrive,
She did not find her dear husband alive.
All that she could find was her husband's blood.
Bitterly she wept, and her tears did flood.

"Oh, my husband dear, see what you have done,
You have gone and orphaned our little ones."
"To my orphans, my dear wife, you will say,
That I lie asleep in America.
Tell them, my dear wife, not to wait for me,
For I lie asleep in America."

Give My Regards To Broadway

From the 1905 Broadway hit show *Little Johnny Jones.*

by George M. Cohan

1. Did you ev - er see two Yan - kees part up - on a
2. Say hel - lo to dear old Co - ney Isle, if there you

for - eign shore;_____ When the good ship's just a -
chance to be;_____ When you're at the Wal - dorf,

bout to start for old New York once more?_____
have a smile and charge it up to me. _____

_ With _ tear - dimmed eye they say good — bye, they're
_ Men-tion my name ev - 'ry place you go, as

You Naughty, Naughty Men

This song predates the songs in this section by at least 30 years. It was the hit song of a musical extravaganza, *The Black Crook,* which opened at Niblo's Gardens in New York in 1866.

Words by T. Kennick
Music by B. Bicknell

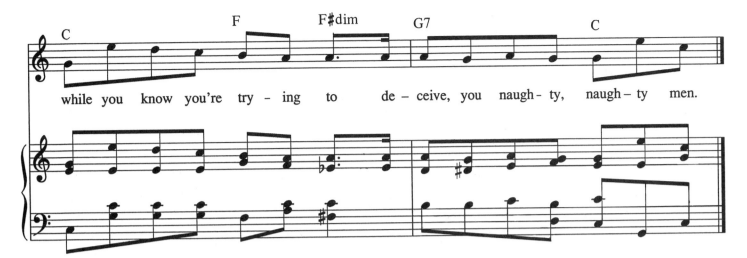

while you know you're try – ing to de – ceive, you naugh – ty, naugh – ty men.

When you want a kiss or favor,
You put on your best behavior,
And your looks of kindness savor,
Oh, you naughty, naughty men;
Of love you set us dreaming,
And when with hope we're teeming,
We find you are but scheming,
You naughty, naughty men.
Of love you set us dreaming,
And when with hope we're teeming,
We find you are but scheming,
You naughty, naughty men.

If a fortune we inherit,
You see in us every merit,
And declare we're girls of **spirit,**
Oh, you naughty, naughty men;
But too often matrimony
Is a mere matter of money,
We get bitters 'stead of honey
From you naughty, naughty men,
But too often matrimony
Is a mere matter of money,
We get bitters 'stead of honey
From you naughty, naughty men.

But with all your faults, we clearly
Love you wicked fellows dearly,
Yes, we dote upon you dearly,
Oh, you naughty, naughty men;
We've no wish to distress you,
We'd sooner far caress you,
And when kind we'll say, "Oh bless you!"
Oh, you naughty, dear, delightful men.
We've no wish to distress you,
We'd sooner far caress you,
And when kind we'll say, "Oh bless you!"
Oh, you naughty, dear, delightful men.

New York Public Library Picture Collection.

Streets Of Cairo

One of the highlights of the 1893 Chicago World's Columbian Exposition was the sensational dance of "Little Egypt." This is a take-off on that dance.

By James Thornton

1. I will sing you a song, And it won't be ver–y long, 'Bout a maid – en sweet, And she nev – er would do wrong. Ev – 'ry – one said she was pret – ty, She was not long in the cit–y,

2. She went out one night, Did this in – no-cent di – vine, With a nice young man Who in – vit – ed her to dine. Now he's sor – ry that he met her, And he nev – er will for – get her,

3. Well, she was en – gaged As a pic – ture for to pose, To ap-pear each night In ab – bre – vi – at – ed clothes. All the dudes were in a flur – ry, For to catch her they did hur – ry,

There'll Be A Hot Time

Words by Joe Hayden
Music by Theodore A. Metz

got   a   rab – bit's foot   to   keep   a – way   the   hoo – doo.
hugged her   and   I   kissed her,   and   to   me   then   she   said,

When   you   hear   that the   preach-ing   does   be – gin,
"Please,   oh,   please,   oh,__   do   not   let   me   fall.

Bend   down   low   for to   drive a – way   your   sin. And   when you
You're   all   mine   and I   love   you   best   of   all;   And   you   must

get   re – li – gion   you__   want   to   shout   and   sing,⎫   There'll be   a
be   my   man__   or   I'll   have   no   man   at   all."⎭

139

The Yankee Doodle Boy

Another hit from *Little Johnny Jones*.

By George M. Cohan

1. I'm the kid that's all the can-dy, I'm a Yan-kee Doo-dle Dan-dy, I'm glad I
2. Fa-ther's name was Hez-e-ki-ah, Moth-er's name was Ann Ma-ri-a, Yanks through and

am, So's Un-cle Sam. I'm a real live Yan-kee Doo-dle, Made my name and
through. Red, White and Blue. Fa-ther was so Yan-kee-heart-ed, When the Span-ish

fame and boo-dle Just like Mis-ter Doo-dle did by rid-ing on a po-ny. I
war was start-ed, He slipped on his u-ni-form and hopped up on a po-ny. My

love to lis-ten to the Dix-ie strain, "I long to see the girl I left be-hind me;" And
moth-er's moth-er was a Yan-kee true, My fa-ther's fa-ther was a Yan-kee, too; And

140

Meet Me In St. Louis, Louis

St. Louis was the site of the 1904 Louisiana Purchase Centennial Exposition.

Words by Andrew Stirling
Music by Kerry Mills

1. When Lou- is came home to the flat,_____ He hung up his
2. The dress- es that hung in the hall_____ Were gone, she had

coat and his hat,_____ He gazed all a- round, but no
ta- ken them all._____ She took all his rings and the

wife- y he found, So he said, "Where can Flos- sie be at?"_____
rest of his things;_____ The pic- ture he missed from the wall._____

___ A note on the ta- ble he spied,_____ He
___ "What! mov- ing?" the jan- i- tor said, "Your

While Strolling Through the Park

By Ed Haley

While__ stroll-ing through the park one day, In the mer-ry month of May, I was tak-en by sur-prise by a pair of ro-guish eyes, In a mo-ment my poor heart was stole a—way. A smile was all she gave to me. Of

course it made me hap – py as can be.

Ah! I im – me – di – ate – ly raised my hat, And

made a po – lite re – mark; I nev – er shall for- get the

love – ly af - ter-noon I met her at the foun – tain in the park.

Down In Dear Old Greenwich Village

Artists and writers always seemed to be attracted to Greenwich Village in Manhattan. Bobby Edwards wrote songs about the "Bohemian life," and sang them at Polly's restaurant on MacDougal Street. This one was published in 1912.

Words By Bobby Edwards

Way down south in Green - wich Vil - lage, That's the field for cul – ture's till - age.

There they have ar – tis - tic rav – ings, Tea and oth – er aw – ful crav - ings.

There the in - spi – ra – tion stops, And they start sil – ly lit – tle shops; You'll

find them an - y – where 'round Wash-ing- ton Square. _____

Down in dear old Greenwich Village,
There they wear no fancy frillage,
For the ladies of the Square
All wear smocks and bob their hair.
There they do not think it shocking
To wear stencils for a stocking,
That saves the laundry bills in Washington Square.

Way down South in Greenwich Village,
Where the spinsters come for thrillage.
There they speak of "sex relations"
With the sordid slavic nations.
'Neath the guise of feminism,
Dodging social ostracism,
They get away with much in Washington Square.

Way down South in Greenwich Village,
Where thay all consume distillage,
Where the fashion illustrators,
Flirt with interior decorators.
There the cheap Bohemian fakirs,
And the boys from Wanamakers
Gather "atmosphere" in Washington Square.

Way down South in Greenwich Village,
Where the brains amount to nillage,
Where the girls are unconventional,
And the men are unintentional.
There the girls are self-supporting,
There the ladies do the courting,
The ladies buy the "eats" in Washington Square.

Way down South in Greenwich Village,
Comes a bunch of Uptown swillage.
Folks from Lenox Subway Stations
Come with lurid expectations.
There the Village informalities
Are construed as abnormalities
By the boobs who visit Washington Square.

The Desperado

There was a des – per – a – do from the wild and wool – ly west. He

came in from Chi – ca – go just to give the west a rest. He

wore a big som – bre – ro and two guns be – neath his vest; And ev – 'ry – where he went he gave his

"wah whoop!" A bold, bad man was this des – per – a – do, From

He came to Coney Island just to take in all the sights,
He went up to the loop-the-loop that scaled the tallest heights.
It got him so excited that he shot out all the lights,
And everywhere he went he gave his "wah whoop!" *Chorus*

A great big fat policeman came a-walking down his beat.
He saw the desperado come on trucking down the street.
He took him by the collar and he took him by the seat,
And put him where he couldn't give his "wah whoop!" *Chorus*

Levee workers, Plaquemines Parish, Louisiana, 1935.   *New York Public Library Picture Collection.*

Waiting For The Robert E. Lee

Words by L. Wolfe Gilbert
Music by Lewis F. Muir

1.'Way down on the lev – ee in old Al- a– bam – y, There's dad- dy and mam-
2. The whis-tles are blow – in', the smoke- stacks are show – in', The ropes they are throw-

– my, there's Eph–raim and Sam – my, On a moon – light night you can find __
__ in', ex - cuse me, I'm go – in' To the place where all is har-mon-

__ them all. While they are wait – in', the ban- jos are syn – co- pa- tin'.
__ i - ous, E – ven the preach – er, __ he is the danc – ing teach- er.

What's that they're say – in? __ What's that they're say – in? __ While they keep play-
Have you been down __ there? __ Were you a – round __ there? If ev- er you go __

The Bowery

The Bowery was *the* place to see and be seen in New York in the 1890s. Restaurants, theaters and dance halls abounded. Now we find flop houses and abandoned buildings.

Words by Charles Hoyt
Music by Percy Gaunt

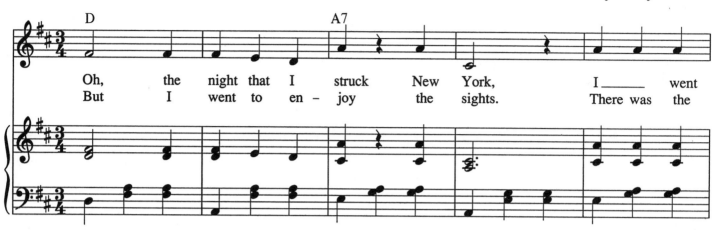

Oh, the night that I struck New York, I _____ went
But I went to en – joy the sights. There was the

out for a qui – et walk. Folks who are on to the
Bow – 'ry a – blaze with lights. I had me one of the

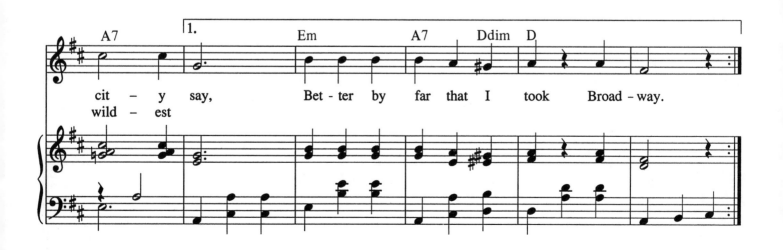

1.

cit – y say, Bet – ter by far that I took Broad – way.
wild – est

156

I had walked but a block or two,
When up came a fellow and me he knew.
Then a policeman came walking by,
Chased him away, and I asked him why.
"Wasn't he pulling your leg?" said he.
Said I, "He never laid hands on me!"
"Get off the Bowery, you fool!" said he.
I'll never go there any more.   *Chorus*

Struck a place that they called a "dive,"
I was in luck to get out alive.
When the policeman, he heard my woes,
Saw my black eyes and my battered nose,
"You've been held up!" then the copper said.
"No, sir! but I've been knocked down instead."
Then he just laughed, though I couldn't see why.
I'll never go there any more.   *Chorus*

Two young females were arrested in 1859 for dressing like men and smoking cigars. They got eight years in a reformatory.
New York Public Library Picture Collection.